LOVE, LIBERTY, AND CHRISTIAN CONSCIENCE

STRIKING THE BIBLICAL BALANCE

RANDY JAEGGLI

UNIVERSITY PRESS

Greenville, South Carolina

Library of Congress Cataloging-in-Publication Data

Jaeggli, Randy, 1952-
   Love, liberty, and Christian conscience : striking the biblical balance /
Randy Jaeggli.
      p. cm.
   Summary: "This book studies the importance of a biblically informed
conscience in developing standards for Christian living"—Provided by
publisher.
   ISBN 978-1-59166-798-8 (perfect bound pbk. : alk. paper)
   1. Conscience—Religious aspects—Christianity. I. Title.
   BJ1278.C66J34 2007
   241'.1—dc22
                                                          2007022022

**Love, Liberty, and Christian Conscience:
Striking the Biblical Balance**

Randy Jaeggli, PhD

Design by Peter Crane
Page layout by Kelley Moore

© 2007 BJU Press
Greenville, South Carolina 29614
Bob Jones University Press is a division of BJU Press

Printed in the United States of America

ISBN 978-1-59166-798-8

15   14   13   12   11   10   9   8   7   6   5   4   3   2   1

to Bob Bell,
my esteemed mentor and friend

CONTENTS

PREFACE

Faithful Christians in every generation hunger for *Biblical Discernment for Difficult Issues*, the title of this book series authored by the faculty of Bob Jones University Seminary. The true disciple thirsts for a life that reflects Christ's love for others while striving to maintain loyalty to God's revealed Truth, the Scriptures. But as every mature Christian soon learns, demonstrating both God's compassion and God's holiness in this life is a balance that is never easy to strike.

Our propensity to wander from the right path is enough to alarm any honest follower of Christ. How quickly in our pursuit of holiness we do race into the darkness of a harsh, unforgiving condemnation of others who somehow lack the light we enjoy. And how tragically inclined we all are to slip, while on the narrow way, from the firm ground of genuine compassion into the mire of an unbiblical naiveté or an unwise sentimentality. Only by God's grace can the believer combine that loving compassion and that pursuit of a rigorous holiness into one life to bring the true "light of the knowledge of the glory of God in the face of Jesus Christ" to a needy church and a lost world.

The aim of this series is to provide help in finding this right, discerning balance in spiritual life without sacrificing one crucial emphasis in Scripture for another. While written in an easy-to-read style, these works attempt to combine mature, penetrating theological thought with thorough research. They aim to provide both a fact-intensive exposition of Scripture and a piercing application of it to real human experience. Hopefully those who read will find themselves making significant strides forward on the way to a renewed mind and a transformed life for the glory of Christ.

Stephen J. Hankins, Dean
Bob Jones University Seminary

1

INTRODUCTION

During the last three summers, my responsibilities have included reading transcripts of chapel messages by Bob Jones Sr.,
from the late 1940s to the mid-1950s. I have recorded what he
said about theological issues so that the library staff can produce
a database for the use of researchers who want to know what the
founder of Bob Jones University believed about a wide range of
biblical issues. Bob Jones was a sentimental man, often reminisc-
ing about his days as a boy in southern Alabama, his ministry
as an evangelist, and the early days of Bob Jones University. He
would sometimes remark with some degree of amazement that
fellow fundamentalists criticized the school for its standards of
Christian conduct more vociferously than theological modernists
condemned the institution for its stance on the essential doctrines
of historic Christianity.

Bob Jones was a practical man who did not care what a man
professed with his mouth if his conduct manifested hypocrisy.
For a person to "drool" piety[1] and then smoke cigarettes, quaff
cocktails, or go to "necking parties" was completely abhorrent to
him. He hated the deleterious influence of Hollywood, especially
the way actors and actresses so readily divorced one another.

---

[1]He said, "Whenever you get filled with pride, even religious pride, the Bible says
something about pride going before destruction. Whenever I get to feeling exception-
ally pious, I wonder if the devil is around, because you know, I'm not naturally any too
pious. It hasn't ever been very easy for me to be pious. I can't drool it like some people."
Archives Room, Mack Library, Bob Jones University, Greenville, SC, p. 11 in the tran-
script of a chapel message dated 10/3/55.

1

He believed a Christian showed his love for his Savior by obeying not just the explicit commands of Scripture but also biblical principles implicitly mandating behavior commensurate with growth in holiness. Every aspect of life was sacred to Bob Jones, from the pastor's task of preaching to the homemaker's responsibilities in maintaining a neat and orderly environment for her family. Love for Christ must produce a lifestyle that honors Him in everything the believer does.

Bob Jones was not the dogmatist that some people imagine. He realized that there is a difference between doctrines that are fundamental to the faith and others that Bible-believing people may disagree about legitimately. He had nothing but scathing denunciation, for instance, for a theologian who would deny the virgin birth of Christ, but he refused to take sides on the Calvinist-Arminian debate. Although he held to the pretribulational rapture of the saints, he understood that good men could differ with him on eschatology and still be his friends. The one thing he could never abide, however, was a traitor to Jesus Christ. For a person claiming saving faith to take the liberty that God gave him through the grace of Christ, and then live in a worldly manner, was to Bob Jones the summit of treachery. In my opinion, he reflected a correct, balanced understanding of the overall teaching of the Scripture in what he believed.

The purpose of this monograph, of course, is not to justify what the founder of a school passionately preached his entire life. The believer's allegiance is ultimately to the Scripture, not to men. As men have preached accurately what the Bible declares, we laud their memory. Unfortunately some leaders, whether pastors or writers, have promoted a warped view of Christian liberty by making outward conformity to a particular set of expected behaviors the test of true spirituality. This sort of externalism ultimately leads to frustration and disillusionment in the lives of believers who are searching for the scriptural path of genuine relationship with Jesus Christ. Other leaders have promoted such a carefree attitude toward the Christian's lifestyle that a follower might legitimately wonder if his life should be outwardly any different from that of an unbeliever. It is difficult these days to find a balanced view. The task before us is to examine with an open heart what the Bible says about love, liberty, and Christian conscience. Because the Lord has established an eternal relationship with believers through salvation in Christ, God has set Christians free from slavery to sin. The thesis of this monograph is that those who are in Christ now enjoy the liberty to love and obey God out of a heart governed by a scripturally informed conscience.

2
MISUNDERSTANDING LEGALISM

In today's wider evangelicalism many leaders are taking an unbalanced view of Christian liberty. They argue that anyone who restricts a believer's liberty in any way that goes beyond explicit prohibitions of Scripture is a legalist. One of the high-profile advocates of this idea is Charles R. Swindoll. As past president and now chancellor of the influential Dallas Theological Seminary, he has the ear of vast numbers of people who would claim salvation by grace through faith in Christ. In his book *The Grace Awakening* he warns his readers that "there are grace killers on the loose!" Swindoll admits that he used to be one of these heinous individuals. "Legalism was my security, and making certain that others marched to my cadence was a major part of my daily agenda."[1] Notice the striking way he uses the word *legalism*.

THE HISTORICAL USE OF LEGALISM

Historically the term *legalism* has been used to describe the idea that a person can obtain salvation through fastidious adherence to a particular code of law, whether Mosaic or manmade. A. R. G. Deasley noted that the term *legalism* "appears to have had a theological origin in the seventeenth century, when Edward Fisher used it to designate 'one who bringeth the Law into the case of Justification' (*The Marrow of Modern Divinity*,

---

[1] Charles R. Swindoll, *The Grace Awakening* (Dallas: Word, 1990), xiv.

1645)."[2] Deasley concluded that legalism is "works done to commend the doer to God. As holding out the hope of salvation on the basis of human effort, such works are the antithesis of God's saving grace set forth in Christ crucified."[3] In 1969, P. S. Watson defined *legalism* as the idea that "man's fulfillment of God's law is the indispensable foundation of man's standing with God."[4] In 1986, Millard J. Erickson defined the term as "a keeping of the law, particularly in a formal sense, and a regarding of obedience as meritorious."[5] Henry W. Holloman, in 2005, maintained that legalism is "any belief that rule-keeping in itself gains merit with God. Legalism teaches that some act of law fulfillment must be added to the work of Christ for salvation or for remaining in a state of salvation."[6]

These definitions mark legalism as an attempt to obtain salvation by works, something that all Bible-believing people find abhorrent. A Pharisee during the time of Christ would qualify as a legalist. Pharisaical righteousness was based on works and involved keeping not only the law of Moses but also the manmade accretions that supposedly kept a person from violating that law. The Pharisee's "righteousness" was an entirely external affair. He thought that as long as he performed all the correct outward actions, he

---

[2]*Evangelical Dictionary of Biblical Theology*, ed. Walter A. Elwell (Grand Rapids: Baker, 1986), s.v. "Legalism," by A. R. G. Deasley, 478.

[3]Ibid., 479.

[4]*A Dictionary of Christian Theology*, ed. Alan Richardson (Philadelphia: Westminster, 1969), s.v. "Legalism," by P. S. Watson, 191. Watson goes on to remark, "It makes no difference whether the requirement of the law is understood in terms of outward conduct or inward motivation, or whether the fulfillment is brought about by man's unaided efforts or by the assistance of grace. The point is that the religious relationship is governed by the law."

[5]*Concise Dictionary of Christian Theology* (Grand Rapids: Baker, 1986), s.v. "Legalism," 95.

[6]*Kregel Dictionary of the Bible and Theology* (Grand Rapids: Kregel, 2005), s.v. "Legalism," 286–87.

must be right with God internally. In a striking simile, Jesus said these Pharisees were like whitewashed sepulchers—beautiful on the outside and full of dead men's bones on the inside (see Matt. 23:27–28).

Of course the Pharisees were entirely mistaken in their understanding of the law. They had no appreciation for the impact of the law in exposing the wretched nature of the human heart. They thought that if they did not commit murder, then they had fulfilled the law's demand. Our Savior condemned this way of thinking by declaring, "Whosoever is angry with his brother without a cause shall be in danger of the judgment" (Matt. 5:22). Similarly the Pharisees congratulated themselves that they had not committed adultery, but Christ said that "whosoever looketh on a woman to lust after her hath committed adultery with her already in his heart" (v. 28).

The Pharisees also had perverted the intent of the law. God did not give the Israelites an external standard of conduct as a means of establishing a righteous standing before Him on the basis of man's obedience. The giving of the law followed God's redemption of His people from Egyptian bondage. His grace accomplished a completely miraculous deliverance based on absolutely no meritorious aspect of the Israelite nation. God instructed His people in the law to appreciate His grace:

> The Lord did not set his love upon you, nor choose you, because ye were more in number than any people; for ye were the fewest of all people: but because the Lord loved you, and because he would keep the oath which he had sworn unto your fathers, hath the Lord brought you out with a mighty hand, and redeemed you out of the house of bondmen, from the hand of Pharaoh king of Egypt. (Deut. 7:7–8)

God gave His law to the Israelites so that they might respond in love to His grace by living in a distinctively different manner from their idolatrous neighbors.[7] This unique lifestyle would bring honor to the one true God, Who desired all mankind to know Him. He therefore commissioned Israel in the law to be "a kingdom of priests, and an holy nation" (Exod. 19:6).

The Pharisees' perversion of the law into a religion of meritorious works rightly occasioned Christ's most scathing denunciation. He had only tender compassion for the vilest of sinners who came to Him in humble trust for the forgiveness of sins, but our Savior warned the self-righteous Pharisees, "Woe unto you, scribes and Pharisees, hypocrites! for ye shut up the kingdom of heaven against men: for ye neither go in yourselves, neither suffer ye them that are entering to go in" (Matt. 23:13). Pharisaic legalism was preventing people from accepting salvation by God's grace. Because they were harming people with eternal perdition, Christ set Himself steadfastly against their doctrine.

The historical use of the term *legalism* can have no proper application to groups that believe in salvation by grace through faith alone. The correct application of the term is in reference to all movements that emphasize adding works to faith, including liberal Protestant denominations and Roman Catholicism in our day. To speak of fundamentalist legalism, in the historic meaning of legalism, creates an oxymoron.[8] I have never heard or read of

---

[7]Deasley states the matter well when he writes, "The narrative setting of the law is essentially an account of God's choosing of Israel to be his people (Gen. 12:1–3; Deut. 1:1–4:49), while the law itself is both a prescriptive statement of the life God expects his people to lead as well as a picture of the kind of life that leads to joy and fulfillment. In short, the law is part of the covenant, and constitutes both God's gracious gift to his people and the vehicle of their grateful response to him (Exod. 19:3–6; Deut. 7:1–16; 26:1–19). This explains the positive picture of the law in the Old Testament" (p. 478).

[8]John F. MacArthur Jr., for example, made this error when he asserted, "In any philosophy that tends to gauge spirituality by external standards—be it *fundamentalist*

any fundamentalist preacher or writer who believes in salvation by works of the law.[9] The Scripture is quite plain that man cannot possibly meet the standard of God's righteousness by his own efforts. Titus 3:5 declares, "Not by works of righteousness which we have done, but according to his mercy he saved us, by the washing of regeneration, and renewing of the Holy Ghost." Galatians 2:16 could hardly make the issue of salvation any clearer: "Knowing that a man is not justified by the works of the law, but by the faith of Jesus Christ, even we have believed in Jesus Christ, that we might be justified by the faith of Christ, and not by the works of the law: for by the works of the law shall no flesh be justified."

The issue of Christian liberty was settled early in the apostolic period at the Jerusalem Council (Acts 15). The meeting of Paul and Barnabas with the church at Jerusalem was necessary because certain men had come from Judea to Antioch and were insisting that circumcision was necessary for salvation (15:1). When sharp dissension at Antioch did not lead to a resolution of the issue, Paul took his cause to the apostles and elders in Jerusalem (vv. 2–4). At Jerusalem Paul encountered a group of Pharisees who had believed

---

legalism, sanctimonious asceticism, communal pietism, religious institutionalism, hard-line pharisaism, wild-eyed mysticism, or rigid monasticism—keeping up appearances tends to take priority over openness and honesty" (emphasis added). *Charismatic Chaos* (Grand Rapids: Zondervan, 1992), p. 21, n. 14. One may note MacArthur's attitude toward fundamentalism by the other groups he places in the same sentence.

[9]Ernest D. Pickering expresses a similar sentiment. In his words, Swindoll "declares that Christian leaders formulate rules of conduct so that persons obeying them can 'earn God's acceptance.' After many years of ministry among thousands of churches both in this country and others, I believe I can say with confidence that I have never met a pastor or Christian leader who believed this. God's acceptance is gained by grace, not through the observance of rules (even biblical ones!). This is an exaggeration which we believe does great disservice to many Christian leaders." *Are Fundamentalists Legalists? A Reply to Charles Swindoll* (no publication information), 15. Dave Doran comes to the same conclusion: "I know of no biblical fundamentalist who is teaching that adhering to a system of personal standards secures their [sic] justification. On the contrary, they very clearly proclaim a gospel of grace that must be received through repentant faith in the person and work of Jesus Christ." "Are Fundamentalists Legalists? Part One," *Frontline* (March/April, 1999), 8–9.

in Christ as their Messiah but were insistent, as the visitors to Antioch had been, that a Gentile must be circumcised and keep the Mosaic law (v. 5).

This emphasis on what *man* must do to merit God's grace was entirely antithetical to Paul's focus on what *God* had done in the lives of Gentiles through his preaching (v. 4). Consultation by the apostles resulted in an agreement not to burden Gentiles with a task that not even the strictest Pharisee had ever been able to accomplish—keeping the law. Peter stated the matter succinctly: "God, which knoweth the hearts, bare them [the Gentiles] witness, giving them the Holy Ghost, even as he did unto us; and put no difference between us and them, purifying their hearts by faith" (vv. 8–9). James then spoke for all the apostles when he concluded that Gentile believers would do well simply to avoid the pollution of idols, fornication, and eating either an animal that had been strangled or blood (vv. 19–20).[10]

It is uncertain why various evangelical leaders use the term *legalist* in reference to fundamentalists. Whether intentionally or not, they use the term as a verbal club to intimidate those who believe in the legitimacy of applying scriptural principles in the development of personal standards of Christian conduct. Sometimes words take on a pejorative connotation when an *-ist* ending is added to a non-threatening term.[11]

---

[10]Interpreters have differed about the significance of these things that are off limits to Christians. It is beyond the scope of this article to explore the issue in depth. It is certain that the main manifestation of an unbelieving heart in the Old Testament was devotion to idolatry. God had commanded His people to have no other gods before Him, but the entire OT recounts one manifestation of idolatry after another. Certain forms of idolatrous worship, such as Baalism, involved cultic prostitution. Many of these idolatrous forms continued into NT times. James was probably warning Gentile believers to avoid the same sort of idolatrous practices that had incurred God's continual judgment on Israel.

[11]Robert D. Bell, "What Is a Legalist?" audiotape of a chapel message at Bob Jones University, 6/26/92.

Consider, for instance, the complimentary term *rational*. It is hard to imagine that anyone would object to being called rational. A Bible-believing Christian, however, would not want to be called a *rationalist*. The *-ist* ending makes the word refer to someone who has gone too far with a particular quality. A rationalist has taken his God-given ability to think logically and has used it as the ultimate measure of truth, even to the point of passing judgment on the truth of God's Word. Similarly any woman would like for someone to say she is *feminine*, but most Christian women would be horrified to be called a *feminist*. The term *legalist* is likewise abhorrent to a true Christian.

The way a person uses words is important because usage determines meaning. If people use a word to mean something different from its historical sense long enough, the meaning of the word actually changes. An example of this process is evident in the translation of 2 Thessalonians 2:7 in the King James Version: "For the mystery of iniquity doth already work: only he who now letteth will let, until he be taken out of the way." When the KJV translators did their work, the verb *to let* meant to restrain someone from doing something. Four hundred years later it means just the opposite. A realization of possible shift in word meaning mandates extreme care in using theological terms with precision. Consequently an orthodox theologian zealously guards the meaning of such terms as *justification, sanctification, grace,* and *faith*. If people start using a term to mean something different from its historic meaning, theological confusion is the result.

THE CURRENT USE OF LEGALISM

This process of change in the meaning of *legalism* is currently taking place. Unless theologians recognize the shift in usage and take corrective measures, the new meaning will become thoroughly entrenched. There are many examples of the contemporary use of the term, but perhaps a few references will suffice.

Swindoll defines the concept as "an attitude, a mentality based on pride. It is an obsessive conformity to an artificial standard for the purpose of exalting oneself."[12] Notice the way his definition removes the term from a precisely soteriological realm. The historical use described an attempt at justification through keeping the objective standard of the Mosaic law. The new definition moves the concept of legalism into a fog bank of obscurity. It is unclear whether "conformity to an artificial standard" relates to justification or sanctification. The nature of the "artificial standard" is opaque, as is the level at which conformity becomes "obsessive." Swindoll goes on to assert that "legalism says, 'I do this or I don't do that, and therefore I am pleasing to God.'"[13] Whatever a person might wish to call the mistaken notion that a Christian can enhance his status as more accepted in the Beloved than he was at the moment of salvation, this is clearly a different idea from the historical use of *legalism*.

Swindoll explains that an "artificial standard" consists of matters that "aren't spelled out in Scripture." He further specifies that "they've been passed down or they have been dictated to the legalist and have become an obsession to him or her."[14] By now it is becoming clear that Swindoll thinks legalism is a mindless and obsessive lifestyle that consists of rote conformity to traditional standards of Christian conduct, with the intent of enhancing a believer's standing with God. Once again, even though the concept Swindoll describes is deplorable Christian living, it is not legalism. In my opinion he is attempting to paint an ugly

---

[12] Swindoll, 81.

[13] Ibid., 81–82.

[14] Ibid., 82.

caricature of the legitimate process of deriving personal standards of Christian conduct from a careful study of the Scripture. He sees only two widely divergent, unbalanced options: (1) live a radically independent, "risky" life controlled by a concept of grace that frees the believer to live apart from rules, or (2) allow oneself to be dominated by a manmade list of do's and don'ts that is "rigid" and "grim."[15] Swindoll's method of argumentation is highly persuasive but, unfortunately, illegitimate.[16] It does not allow for a third, balanced view.

Mark L. Bailey followed Swindoll as president of Dallas Theological Seminary in 2001. In a 1987 article Bailey demonstrates the same confusion about legalism his predecessor manifested. Bailey states, "Originally fought in the arena of salvation, this battle between legalism and license in our century has entered into the arena of sanctification."[17] In order to prove his case, he examines various New Testament passages concerning the error of the Pharisees. He correctly notes that "in the time of Christ, the most notable legalists were the Pharisees."[18] But then he commits a theological sleight of hand. He discusses the Pharisees' problem in a way that blurs the distinction between justification and sanctification, and he proceeds to describe the process by which the Pharisees placed more importance on their manmade additions to the law than on the Word of God itself. He states that these additions to the law, "as well as any other additions

---

[15]Swindoll seems adept at selecting the most negative, evocative language to describe those who establish biblical standards for living (see, e.g., p. 82).

[16]Doran has an interesting discussion of "the fallacy of the excluded middle. This fallacy sets up two extremes as the only options available with no ground left between them." "Are Fundamentalists Legalists? Part Two," *Frontline* (May/June 1999), 14. Doran's two-part series manifests impeccable logic, and it is the most helpful analysis I have found.

[17]"Thou Shalt Not!" *Kindred Spirit* (Autumn 1987), 6.

[18]Ibid.

one might make to the Word of God today," skew our loyalty toward "a superficial standard of external rituals which tend to fog the biblical focus on the internal reality of a genuine relationship with God."[19]

Bailey passes over the key issue: the Pharisees' foundational problem was not their zeal for the law that motivated them to add manmade hedges around God's stipulations, lest they inadvertently break a commandment (Jesus in fact commended them for what they had actually done but condemned them for what they left undone, Matt. 23:23). Their problem was an incorrect view of the law as a means of justification. They were unsaved men bound for hell!

Bailey thus trivializes legalism by asserting that "all of us at some time or another have had the experience of being under club memberships, church covenants, college rules, or Christian 'standards of behavior' that we or someone else would criticize as being legalistic."[20] He apparently sees no difference between the externalism of the lost Pharisees and the practice of believers through the centuries of church history who have internalized the Word of God and applied the Word in establishing standards of godly behavior.

---

[19] Ibid., 6–7.

[20] Ibid., 5. To be fair, not all evangelicals have accepted the idea that college rules are legalistic. Zane C. Hodges, for example, reminisces, "When I did my undergraduate work at Wheaton College, like all other Wheaton students, I signed the famous Wheaton pledge. The pledge, of course, bound me to abstain from things like drinking, smoking, dancing, card playing, and going to movies. To many people today, that kind of policy smacks of a very bad case of legalism. Yet I am happy to report that I never had a problem with the Wheaton pledge at all. Not only did I abstain from all these things while a student there, but I was actually glad the pledge existed. In my humble opinion, the Wheaton pledge was a good idea for a Christian school and was in no small degree responsible for creating a good atmosphere on campus. . . . Naturally there were some people, even in those days, who thought the Wheaton pledge was a par excellence example of rigid fundamentalism with its so-called legalistic mentality. This accusation, however, was false." "Legalism: the Real Thing," *Journal of the Grace Evangelical Society* (Autumn 1996), 21–22.

The current evangelical interest in branding Christian standards as legalistic has sometimes produced arguments that are culpably superficial. In his article "The Trouble with Legalism," Leith Anderson begins with a story about Bob, who has been praying that his friend Rich will be saved. The night Bob hopes to lead Rich to Christ, Rich shows up at the door with a present to show his appreciation for Bob's friendship: a nice bottle of wine. Now Bob is in a real quandary because he is a leader in a church that requires abstinence from alcoholic beverages. Anderson's conclusion to the story is that "no matter how many rules we have, there are never enough."[21] So rather than having Bob simply say, "Thank you," to Rich, ask him into his home, and present the gospel to him, Anderson supposes that he has created a scenario that requires the wisdom of Solomon to resolve.

Even a casual reader of this account realizes that Bob had at least three options. His first option would have been to thank Rich for his thoughtful gift and explain kindly that he does not drink alcoholic beverages. His second possible recourse would have been to open the bottle of wine after Rich had left, pour it into a mason jar, and use it for cooking purposes. His third option would have been simply to pour the wine down the drain in his kitchen sink after Rich had departed. In any event Bob did not have to offend Rich, nor did he have to violate a clear and necessary stipulation for his position of leadership at church. (Later we'll demonstrate that Bob's choices will depend, among other things, on his own conscience.)

Anderson maintains that "we are all legalists at heart."[22] He states that all humans display this tendency to run their lives by making rules for everything, even a professional baseball player who

---

[21] *Moody* (October 1994), 13.

[22] Ibid.

always goes through the same superstitious ritual when he comes to bat! The cure for this legalism, according to Anderson, is God's grace. "Practically, this means minimizing the rules and maximizing the grace. We open up to God's goodness and generosity that come to us whether we keep rules or not."[23]

Many Christians in wider evangelicalism are following Anderson's idea that the way of freedom and blessing is to jettison standards of conduct. Social drinking, viewing movies with salacious content, listening to various genres of music with sensual appeal, and a desire for material prosperity that eclipses commitment to the local church are becoming more common. After all, if there are no rules for the Christian life outside of very specific biblical prohibitions, then there is no standard by which much of someone's conduct may be judged correct or incorrect, fruitful or barren. Worldliness and sin, except those sins explicitly condemned in Scripture, become meaningless concepts. All that remains is a blissful ignorance that the believer may be living in self-indulgence and disobedience, lacking self-control and discipline.

Anderson even confuses disciplined living with legalism. He tells the story of Mike, who followed the advice of others in adhering to a schedule that would keep him on track to read the Bible through in one year. "Though there is no such prescription from God, Mike legalistically obeyed. He learned little, however, and increasingly hated the discipline." Finally, "Mike prayed for God's release, quit his legalistic Bible reading, and accepted God's grace. The results were wonderful."[24] This is how far things have progressed in evangelicalism; now even adhering to a Bible-reading schedule is legalistic. Sadly, Leith Anderson is not an obscure person whose opinions matter little. He is the pastor of Wooddale Church in

---

[23] Ibid., 14.
[24] Ibid.

Eden Prairie, Minnesota, a church with thousands in attendance each week. His voice is heard across America on a radio broadcast called "Faith Matters."[25]

Perhaps the most chilling idea about legalism involves the false dichotomy that current usage creates between the establishment of standards of Christian conduct and the ministry of the Holy Spirit in a believer's life.[26] David R. Miller promotes the idea that rules and the work of the Spirit are incompatible: "Legalism leaves little room for love and mercy in dealing with misbehavior. It has no room at all for the guidance of the Holy Spirit as we lead our families. Who needs the Holy Spirit when we have absolute rules to guide us?"[27]

In order to illustrate the harm legalism can wreak on the Christian home, Miller implies that one's only choice is between authoritarianism and the control of the Spirit. He gives an example of what he considers legalistic reasoning in relation to what kind of music a Christian parent should allow in his home: since heavy metal music is bad, and guitars are used to play this rock genre, then no parent ought to allow his child to have any contact with a guitar. Miller says that the legalistic parent whose child rebels against this line of reasoning is likely to lock him in the fruit cellar or send him to Texas. The net effect of legalistic parenting is to banish the Holy Spirit from Christian homes and to run them "like Marine boot camps."[28] Miller concludes his article by asserting that he has

---

[25]Available from http://wooddale.org/guest_center/history/history4.asp; accessed 17 July 2006.

[26]Mark Sidwell has observed that a "common tactic used to argue against separation is to set it against another biblical teaching. Opponents of separation, in other words, formulate dichotomies. . . . The problem, as we will see, is that the arguments being used are false dichotomies." *The Dividing Line: Understanding and Applying Biblical Separation* (Greenville, SC: BJU Press, 1998), 11.

[27]"Legalism: The Tie That Binds and Gags, A Personal Story," *Fundamentalist Journal* (July/August 1988), 33.

[28]Ibid., 34.

reaped a tremendous benefit through repudiating legalism: "We have regained the leadership of the Holy Spirit in our work as Christian parents."[29]

Miller's bombastic style, in which he uses the most absurd charges he can think of (regardless of whether any real evidence exists of Christian parents locking their children in fruit cellars), provides yet another example of a common trait among those who wish to redefine the concept of legalism: they present two widely divergent options and ignore the possibility of a third, balanced view. Miller does not consider the possibility of relying on the Holy Spirit's ministry of illumination through the exegetically sound and carefully applied use of the Scripture in developing standards for personal conduct.

A key doctrine since the time of the Reformation, illumination is the action of the indwelling Holy Spirit in the believer's life whereby the Christian understands the spiritual significance of the Scripture—in contrast to the unsaved person, who sees biblical teaching ultimately as foolishness (1 Cor. 2:6–16).[30] The Holy Spirit uses the Word that He inspired to direct the lives of Christians who rely on Him and study the Bible with a zealous intent to obey. Illumination produces discernment, and discernment must affect the countless choices the believer makes every day. If Christianity is not powerful enough to transform both the inner man *and* his outward actions, our faith is nothing but a mystical delusion—no different from all other impotent, false religions that

---

[29] Ibid., 35.

[30] Henry C. Thiessen writes, "The one who inspired men in the writing of Scripture, illumines the minds of those who read it. Because of sin and the darkened understanding brought about because of sin, no one can understand Scripture properly (Rom. 1:21; Eph. 4:18). But the Spirit can enlighten the mind of the believer to understand the Scriptures. This is the burden of 1 Cor. 2:6–16." *Lectures in Systematic Theology*, rev. Vernon D. Doerksen (Grand Rapids: Eerdmans, 1979), 63.

have held mankind in bondage for millennia. The very heart and soul of biblical Christianity is being threatened by those who re-define the concept of legalism and conclude that grace frees them to live however they wish.

3

THE ROLE OF CONSCIENCE

One of the main roadblocks to the idea that Christian living is at its best in the absence of standards of conduct is the biblical revelation concerning the role of conscience in the believer's life. Of course one's conscience can lead him astray if it is misinformed. I was raised in the home of a former World War II PT boat commander. He ran our household in some ways as if the war were still being waged. We would never think of buying something made in Japan. If my mother happened inadvertently to serve bread with some mold on it, Dad would simply cut out the affected part and declare that mold was healthful. He had eaten far worse than that in the navy! If we didn't eat every crumb of food on our plates, it was a big deal, and he made us sit at the table until we finished the entire meal. I can remember one episode of staring at a serving of cooked carrots for several hours before amassing enough courage to choke them down. So even to this day, decades later, my conscience tells me that I must eat everything on my plate—no matter how huge a portion a waiter at a restaurant has just served me. Only recently have I developed the ability to stop eating when I'm full and just take the remainder home in a box. My conscience still bothers me (slightly) that I own two cars made by Japanese manufacturers. A badly informed conscience can produce unwelcome results.

CONSCIENCE GUARDS THE HEART

A conscience that has been informed by carefully interpreted Scripture, however, is of inestimable value. It seems strange that one rarely hears or reads much about this important guardian of the Christian's heart. John F. MacArthur Jr., laments in his book *The Vanishing Conscience* that those who espouse principles of popular psychology have been successful in convincing many believers that their guilt feelings are better explained as a syndrome than as a consequence of sin. Modern believers have been told that sin is an old-fashioned concept, and now the notions of disease or codependency are preferable. It seems that no one is personally responsible for anything he or she does. People increasingly blame their parents or a poor environment for their sinful actions. The effect of this overemphasis on psychology is to make the concept of sin, and the guilt feelings it produces, foreign to the way people think. Then the message of salvation from sin through the vicarious sacrifice of Christ makes no sense. The gospel seems simply quaint or anachronistic, and the gnawing guilt of sin that the conscience produces in the human heart continues unabated.[1]

What the Word *Heart* Means

When a person hears the English word *heart*, he usually thinks of the seat of human emotion. Someone might say concerning a particularly empathetic person, "He has a big heart." Although the biblical concept includes the idea of emotion, the Scripture uses the word *heart* to describe a broader concept. The Hebrew word for heart (*leb*) refers to the entirety of the inner person.[2] Although the Hebrews did not have a penchant for dissecting the inner as-

---

[1]John F. MacArthur Jr., *The Vanishing Conscience* (Nashville: Nelson, 1995). Note MacArthur's solemn warning: "Where there is no recognition of sin and guilt, when the conscience has been abused into silence, there can be no salvation, no sanctification, and therefore no real emancipation from sin's ruthless power" (p. 34).

[2]"In its abstract meanings, 'heart' became the richest biblical term for the totality of man's inner or immaterial nature. In biblical literature it is the most frequently used term for man's immaterial personality functions as well as the most inclusive term for them since, in the Bible, virtually every immaterial function of man is attributed to the 'heart.'" Andrew Bowling, "*leb, lebab*," *Theological Wordbook of the Old Testament*, ed. R. Laird Harris (Chicago: Moody, 1980), 1:466.

pects of man's being, many times a person's *intellectual* capacity is the primary focus of *leb*. Genesis 6:5, for instance, declares that men before the flood were wicked in their thinking: "And God saw that the wickedness of man was great in the earth, and that every imagination of the thoughts of his heart was only evil continually." The heart is the origin of what a person thinks, as Christ asserted when He said, "But those things which proceed out of the mouth come forth from the heart" (Matt. 15:18). Although it is not the primary focus, the biblical concept of the heart also includes *emotional* aspects. In the verse immediately following the description of man's wicked thinking, Moses records that God's heart was grieved over the depth of human depravity (Gen. 6:6). The third aspect of the heart is its ability to fix itself steadfastly on a certain course of action as an activity of the *will*. The Chronicler says of Rehoboam, for instance, that "he did evil, because he prepared not his heart to seek the Lord" (2 Chron. 12:14).

The Origin of the Heart and Conscience

Man's heart, the totality of his inner being, is created by God. Man has the ability to reason, to express emotion, and to make decisions because he is made in God's image: "And God said, Let us make man in our image, after our likeness" (Gen. 1:26). The Hebrew words for *image* and *likeness* are synonyms[3] and describe a model of something. When the Philistines captured the ark of the covenant after the Israelites had foolishly taken it into battle, God began to plague the enemies of Israel so that many of them suffered from tumors and died. When the Philistines finally sent the ark back to Israel, they included images of the tumors and mice that had afflicted them. The image, a three-dimensional model,

---

[3]Charles Caldwell Ryrie states, "Though some have attempted to make a distinction between the two words to teach two aspects of the image of God, no sharp distinction between them can be sustained linguistically." *Basic Theology: A Popular Systematic Guide to Understanding Biblical Truth* (Chicago: Moody, 1999), 217.

was not the real thing, but it looked enough like the actual item that one could tell something about the plagues God had sent (1 Sam. 5:1–6:18).

To say that Adam and Eve were created in the image of God, then, does not mean that they were divine but that they manifested God's character as fully as finite creatures can reflect infinite perfections. God is omniscient, so Adam and Eve displayed impressive *intellectual* capacity. As the original biologist, Adam had the ability to name every living being in one day.[4] The intellectual, emotional, and volitional aspects of man's inner being are the result of divine creation. Before Adam plunged the human race into sin, every thought of his heart was commensurate with what God would think. Every word from his mouth was a word that God would speak. Every action was pleasing to God and in full accord with the divine will.

Adam and Eve also manifested a *will*—a volitional commitment to obey God's command concerning the prohibition against eating the fruit of the tree of the knowledge of good and evil. God had clearly enunciated this prohibition to Adam: "Of every tree of the garden thou mayest freely eat: but of the tree of the knowledge of good and evil, thou shalt not eat of it: for in the day that thou eatest thereof thou shalt surely die" (Gen. 2:16–17). Eve demonstrated that conscience was at work even before the Fall. When the serpent questioned Eve about the prohibition God had given, he insinuated that God was overly restrictive: "Yea, hath God said, Ye shall not eat of every tree of the garden?" (3:1).[5] Eve responded

---

[4]To say that Adam named all living beings in one day does not mean, of course, that he assigned a genus and species to each one. He may have grouped together various organisms with shared characteristics and given them a general name. Still, his feat was amazing.

[5]The serpent's words may be translated in two possible ways: (1) as the KJV does, and (2) as most modern translations do. The NASB, for instance, translates, "Did God

by quoting what God had told Adam: "We may eat of the fruit of the trees of the garden: but of the fruit of the tree which is in the midst of the garden, God hath said, Ye shall not eat of it, neither shall ye touch it, lest ye die" (3:2–3).

The majority of commentators on this passage, in my opinion, miss the correct interpretation of what is happening by reading too much into several aspects of Eve's answer to the serpent's challenge that God has been overly restrictive. First, they assert that Eve's failure to state that she and Adam could eat freely from the trees of the garden shows her preoccupation with the injunction concerning the one tree they could not enjoy.[6] Second, they say that Eve's addition, "neither shall ye touch it," shows her resentment to God's original command.[7] Third, they think that Eve's weakening of the consequences

---

really say, 'You must not eat from *any* tree in the garden'?" (emphasis added). The difference between "every" and "any" is found in the possible meanings of the Hebrew word *kol*. William L. Holladay states that when *kol* is used with the *min* preposition (as in Gen. 3:1), the meaning is "from no tree at all." *A Concise Hebrew and Aramaic Lexicon of the Old Testament* (Grand Rapids: Eerdmans, 1971), 157. Thus the serpent's initial appeal to Eve involved an absurd overstatement of God's prohibition in order to focus undue attention on the one actual prohibition. Victor P. Hamilton correctly observes that the serpent "grossly exaggerates God's prohibition, claiming that God did not allow them access to any of the orchard trees. Apart from this claim being unadulterated distortion, it is an attempt to create in the woman's mind the impression that God is spiteful, mean, obsessively jealous, and self-protective." *The Book of Genesis: Chapters 1–17*, The New International Commentary on the Old Testament, ed. Robert L. Hubbard (Grand Rapids: Eerdmans, 1990), 188–89.

[6]H. C. Leupold displays this thinking when he states, "Eve emphasizes the fact that God had allowed them to eat of the fruit of the trees of the garden. But a significant omission in her statement of the case must be noted. The original charter of privileges under this head (2:16) had carried the word 'all'; then followed the one exception. Eve omits the 'all.' She was beginning to lose sight of the boundless goodness of God. Apparently, *there sin took its beginning*" (emphasis added). *Exposition of Genesis* (Grand Rapids: Baker, 1942), 1:148.

[7]Leupold develops this assertion in some detail: "Nowhere has it been indicated that God said: 'nor touch it.' By this insertion Eve betrays the course her thoughts have taken. She feels that the prohibition was unduly sharp, so unconsciously she sharpens it herself. But, again, already the attitude of the heart to God is clearly seen no longer to be one of perfect trust" (p. 148). For similar statements see also Henry M. Morris, *The Genesis Record: A Scientific and Devotional Commentary on the Book of Beginnings* (Grand Rapids: Baker, 1976), 111; Hamilton, 189; John J. Davis, *Paradise to Prison:*

of disobedience shows her nonchalant attitude. They note that Eve did not assert she and Adam would *surely die* if they disobeyed God, as God had stated in 2:17, but only that they *might* die.[8]

In answer to these three charges that Eve is already in the process of falling into sin when she utters the words of 3:2–3, one must insist that Eve did not have to give a verbatim quotation of God's injunction in order to demonstrate that she believed it. Her paraphrase of God's words to Adam, in my opinion, shows that she had truly internalized and understood the essence of what God had commanded. This explains why Eve's assertion, "We may eat of the fruit of the trees of the garden," is a wholly adequate understanding of God's permission to enjoy the bounty of Eden.

Concerning Eve's addition, "neither shall ye touch it," interpreters do not even consider that Moses may have chosen not to record the phrase in 2:17 for the purpose of enhancing the reader's surprise when Eve states it in 3:3. I could find only one commentator who noted that the Hebrew verb translated "touch" does not convey the exact semantic equivalent of the English word.[9] The English translation promotes the idea that Eve could violate God's command simply by reaching out her fingers and coming into contact with the fruit. Although the Hebrew verb *nega'* can refer to simple physical

---

Studies in Genesis (Grand Rapids: Baker, 1975), 88; Harold G. Stigers, *A Commentary on Genesis* (Grand Rapids: Zondervan, 1976), 73; and Bill T. Arnold, *Encountering the Book of Genesis* (Grand Rapids: Baker, 1998), 36.

[8]Martin Luther believed that this was the point at which Eve turned from faith to unbelief. *Lectures on Genesis Chapters 1–5*, trans. George V. Schick, in *Luther's Works, Volume 1*, ed. Jaroslav Pelikan (St. Louis: Concordia, 1958), 155. Alan P. Ross is representative of many modern commentators who assert that "'Lest you die' carries the meaning of God's warning, but it does not clearly retain the certainty of the penalty of death." *Creation and Blessing: A Guide to the Study and Exposition of Genesis* (Grand Rapids: Baker, 1988), 135.

[9]See U. Cassuto, *A Commentary on the Book of Genesis, Part I, From Adam to Noah*, trans. Israel Abrahams (Jerusalem: The Magnes Press, 1961), 145. Cassuto concludes that the phrase *neither shall you touch it* is synonymous with the Lord's injunction in 2:17, "You shall not eat thereof."

contact, as in Leviticus 5:2, it often describes the much stronger action of striking at someone with the intent of harming him.[10]

Moses clearly used the verb in this way when he recounted the words of Abimelech to Isaac: "Let there be now an oath betwixt us, even betwixt us and thee, and let us make a covenant with thee; That thou wilt do us no hurt, as we have not touched thee" (Gen. 26:28–29). Considering this stronger use of the verb, "to touch" the fruit of the tree would be to harm it by biting into it and devouring it. The action would be synonymous to eating the fruit. Apparently, then, Eve has stated the prohibition God gave Adam in its full form of synonymous Hebrew parallelism.

The third misunderstanding, that Eve weakened God's prohibition by introducing conditionality into the consequence of disobedience, involves some exploration of Hebrew syntax. Truly God's original statement to Adam involved the strongest language possible in expressing the certainty of death as the consequence of disobedience. "Thou shalt surely die" (2:17) is the translation of the infinitive absolute of *muth* followed by the finite verb of the same source.[11] When Eve restates the prohibition to the serpent by using the phrase *lest ye die* (3:3), she uses the conjunction *pen* with the imperfect of *muth*. In the Hebrew verb transformation system, this use of the imperfect could be modal: "lest you might die." But the syntactical construction with the imperfect can also convey the certainty of what will happen in the future.[12]

---

[10]R. K. Harrison and I. Swart note, "In some passages the vb. specifically denotes the idea of striking someone with the intention to harm or kill, or to inflict a disastrous blow upon that person." "*nega*'," in *New International Dictionary of Old Testament Theology and Exegesis*, ed. Willem A. VanGemeren (Grand Rapids: Zondervan, 1997), 3:24.

[11]See *Gesenius' Hebrew Grammar*, ed. E. Kautzsch, rev. A. E. Cowley (Oxford: Clarendon Press, 1910), paragraph 113n, p. 342.

[12]See Michael P. V. Barrett and Robert D. Bell, *Bob Jones Seminary Hebrew Handbook*, 5th ed. (Greenville, SC: Bob Jones University Press, 2002), 52–55.

Additionally, the conjunction *pen* does not always introduce conditionality. With the imperfect it can convey the "prevention of an otherwise predictable event."[13] In other words, the construction may be translated "otherwise you will die." As a completely adequate paraphrase of God's injunction, this latter option makes the best sense. Genesis 3:3 should be translated, "But from the fruit of the tree which is in the middle of the garden, God said, 'You must not eat from it, and you must not touch it—otherwise you will die.'" There is no conditionality in Eve's thinking about the consequence of disobedience.

If this interpretation is correct, the reader of the Genesis narrative has had an encounter with the mysterious guardian of the human heart called conscience. The reader gets a glimpse of a perfect human being, with a conscience informed by a proper understanding of the word and will of God, taking a stand against the satanic temptation to view God's will as overly restrictive.[14] Man's conscience existed before sin entered the world, and both man's heart and his conscience are essential aspects of the image of God. Clearly man's conscience alone cannot keep a person from sinning, and acting against one's conscience produces disastrous consequences. Eve acted in violation of her conscience and the divine image in which she was created when she believed the serpent's lying words, "Ye shall not surely die" (3:4).[15]

It is unclear why Eve so readily believed the serpent. Since it had never crossed her mind to lie, perhaps she could not conceive

---

[13] Holladay, 293.

[14] There would not be another perfect human in the same circumstance until our Savior faced the same satanic temptation, only with a victorious outcome (Matt. 4:1–11).

[15] James Montgomery Boice correctly concludes that Eve did not fall into sin until she believed Satan's lie and manifested her unbelief in God's word by eating of the forbidden fruit. *Genesis 1:1–11:32*, vol. 1 of *Genesis: An Expositional Commentary* (Grand Rapids: Zondervan, 1982), 135.

of anyone saying anything that was not true. Having been deceived, she then lusted after the forbidden fruit and sinned by eating it (3:6; see 1 Tim. 2:14 and James 1:14–15). She believed the serpent's lie that benefit would accrue to her if she violated what her conscience knew. The serpent promised that she would be like God, but ironically she had already been like God by virtue of being created in His image. The serpent promised that she would know good and evil, but, once again, the creation that God had pronounced good repeatedly in Genesis 1 had always been available for her careful study. God had intended for Eve to know evil simply as the opposite of good, but now she came to know evil experientially. She had taken to herself the divine prerogative as ultimate judge of right and wrong,[16] but her new condition brought only misery and death instead of the benefit the serpent had promised.

The Relation of Heart and Conscience

Although no Hebrew word for *conscience* appears in the OT, one can see the operation of conscience repeatedly. The first thing Adam and Eve did after eating the forbidden fruit, for example, was to sew fig leaves together to hide their nakedness. The concept of hiding was popular that day; Adam and Eve then hid themselves from God's presence. Their consciences produced a sense of guilt, the awareness that their action of disobedience did not match the standard of obedience they knew in their heart. God had told Adam clearly that he was not to eat from that one tree, even though he was at liberty to feast on the fruit from all the other trees of the garden. In Eden before the Fall, there was a perfect balance between liberty and prohibition. Since Adam and Eve loved their Creator and

---

[16]Hamilton describes Eve's condition well: "Whenever one makes his own will crucial and God's revealed will irrelevant, whenever autonomy displaces submission and obedience in a person, that finite individual attempts to rise above the limitations imposed on him by his creator" (p. 190).

enjoyed His fellowship, surely obedience to one injunction was not onerous. Imagine therefore how the guilt of sin must have produced fear in the presence of their holy God. Here is the first evidence in Scripture of conscience condemning human sin. It is a tragic aspect of the blinding quality of sin, however, that the dissonance between Adam's conscience and his action of disobedience produced nothing more than the fabrication of an excuse: he maintained that Eve was the ultimate culprit (Gen. 3:12). Adam was really implying that God Himself was ultimately to blame for providing Eve as Adam's companion and helper.

The close connection between man's heart and his conscience is evident in the OT narrative of David's action of cutting off a piece of Saul's robe (1 Sam. 24:1–22). The narrative begins with the report to Saul that David and his men have been hiding in the wilderness of En-gedi. Saul chose no less than three thousand of his best soldiers and set out to hunt David like a trophy animal. Along the way Saul had to relieve himself, so in God's providence he sought privacy in the very cave where David and his men were hiding. The low probability that such a circumstance could happen without divine intervention was not lost on David's men: "Behold, this is the day of which the Lord said to you, 'Behold; I am about to give your enemy into your hand, and you shall do to him as it seems good to you'" (24:4, NASB). It is unlikely that David's men are referring here to some unknown past prophecy from the Lord that David would someday put Saul to death. Rather they surmise that the providential events of the day are actually a form of divine revelation to David that the Lord has granted him permission to kill the king.[17]

---

[17]Keil and Delitzsch note that David's men "regarded the leadings of providence by which Saul had been brought into David's power as a divine intimation to David himself to take this opportunity of slaying his deadly enemy, and called this intimation a word of Jehovah." C. F. Keil and F. Delitzsch, *Biblical Commentary on the Books of Samuel*, trans. James Martin (Grand Rapids: Eerdmans, rpt. 1978), 235.

Emboldened by the certainty of his men, David sneaks up on Saul. The reader will never know whether David intended to kill Saul because David cut off the corner of Saul's robe instead of doing him bodily harm. The modern reader is surprised by the narrator's next statement: "And it came to pass afterward, that David's heart smote him, because he had cut off Saul's skirt" (v. 5). Today's reader is likely to wonder why such a seemingly small misdeed would result in such a huge consequence.

The Hebrew verb translated "smote" is *nakah*, a verb that describes a lethal or severely debilitating blow.[18] One might translate the phrase, "And the heart of David dealt him a devastating blow" (v. 6 in Hebrew). Notice that modern English versions understand this idiom to be a function of conscience. The NASB, for example, translates the verse, "And it came about afterward that David's *conscience bothered him* because he had cut off the edge of Saul's robe" (emphasis added). David's action was actually a form of rebellion against his king.[19] The Lord had placed Saul on the throne of Israel, and Saul was to remain there until God Himself removed him. When David showed rebellious contempt for God-ordained authority, his conscience brought overwhelming feelings of guilt. Conscience acts as the internal judge of every thought and decision of the human heart.

---

[18] J. Conrad's thorough analysis of the word shows that most often the subject of the verb is a human or Yahweh. "Only rarely are other entities the subject of *nkh*; in all these cases the verb is used figuratively. . . . The subject of *nkh* can be the conscience (*leb*; NRSV: heart), which figuratively hurts or punishes a guilty person." "*nkh*," in *Theological Dictionary of the Old Testament*, ed. G. Johannes Botterweck, Helmer Ringgren, and Heinz-Josef Fabry, trans. David E. Green (Grand Rapids: Eerdmans, 1998), 9:422.

[19] "In cutting off the corner of Saul's robe, David may have been symbolically depriving Saul of his royal authority and transferring it to himself." Ronald F. Youngblood, "1, 2 Samuel," in *The Expositor's Bible Commentary*, ed. Frank E. Gaebelein (Grand Rapids: Zondervan, 1992), 3:746. Youngblood bases his interpretation on "parallels with cuneiform texts found at Mari and Alalakh."

Conscience Judges Outward Actions

In Romans 2:15 Paul further develops this idea of the conscience (the Greek noun is *suneidēsis*) as an internal judge of a man's outward actions. In developing the truth that all mankind is guilty before God, Paul asserts that God will judge Gentiles, who have never had access to the Mosaic law, by an internal law produced through the operation of conscience. Of course no man is justified by the works of the law (Gal. 2:16), but Paul asserts that God has built into man's heart an awareness of what is right and wrong. The Gentiles "shew the work of the law written in their hearts, their conscience also bearing witness, and their thoughts the mean while accusing or else excusing one another" (Rom. 2:15). This verse is important to our study because it corroborates the truth that every man, as a result of his creation in the image of God, has an innate understanding about Who God is and what He requires in human conduct. Whether a person is Jew or Gentile, therefore, conscience is always at work evaluating the moral quality of one's actions.[20]

At times the Scripture informs us that this internal judge of outward actions can be misinformed, and therefore inaccurate, either in its condemnation of an acceptable action or commendation of a wrong one. This is not at all surprising, because man's fall into sin marred the image of God in him.

In 1 Corinthians 8 Paul describes an oversensitive conscience as *weak*.[21] Since Paul has been addressing questions about which the

---

[20]"What God has written on his heart finds a response in man's conscience. . . . It is that individual's inner sense of right and wrong; his (to a certain extent divinely imparted) moral consciousness viewed in the act of pronouncing judgment upon himself, that is, upon his thoughts, attitudes, words, and deeds, whether past, present, or contemplated." William Hendriksen, *New Testament Commentary: Exposition of Paul's Epistle to the Romans* (Grand Rapids: Baker, 1980), 1:97.

[21]The Greek term for *weak* is *asthenēs*. This is a general term that can refer to physical maladies, any weakness in general, something that is simply unimpressive or less

believers at Corinth had asked him (beginning in 1 Cor. 7:1), the reader is not sure whether the term *weak* in 1 Corinthians 8:7 is Paul's word or the Corinthians'.

Whatever the case, within the book of 1 Corinthians, Paul has used the term ironically in passages leading up to his discussion of the weak conscience in 8:7. Paul stated in his first use of the term that "the weakness of God is stronger than men" (1 Cor. 1:25). Of course there is no weakness in divine omnipotence, but even the smallest display of God's power would unveil a strength far superior to man's. Irony is a powerful figure of speech requiring the reader to understand that the author actually means the opposite of what his words say. In 1:27 the apostle has affirmed, "God hath chosen the weak things of the world to confound the things which are mighty." Here the sense of irony is subtle, because Christians really are just as weak as any unsaved person in terms of ability to merit salvation. The irony in 1:27 involves the wrong view the world has concerning believers. Worldly people think they are strong and Christians are weak, but God's work of salvation results in just the opposite situation.

In 4:10, however, the irony of Paul's words is unmistakable: "We are fools for Christ's sake, but ye are wise in Christ; we are weak, but ye are strong." Paul does not actually consider himself a fool; as he already stated in 1:30, "But of him are ye in Christ Jesus, who of God is made unto us *wisdom*, and righteousness, and sanctification, and redemption" (emphasis added). Paul makes it clear in other passages as well that he really is not weak (see for instance 4:18–21).

So when the reader encounters the term *weak* in 8:7, he wonders whether Paul might not be speaking with his tongue in his

---

important, or moral weakness. See Walter Bauer, *A Greek-English Lexicon of the New Testament and Other Early Christian Literature*, trans. William F. Arndt and F. Wilbur Gingrich (Chicago: The University of Chicago Press, 1957), 115.

cheek. Perhaps the real problem is that certain Corinthian believers have a conscience that is actually too strong, or—to phrase it another way—oversensitive, because it has not been informed by the Word of God. These hypersensitive believers, so unbalanced that they would eat no meat at all (lest they unknowingly eat food that had been sacrificed to idols), were a continual aggravation to other Christians at Corinth who were so unbalanced toward liberty that they would actually dine at feasts in an idol's temple. One can only imagine the magnitude of verbal warfare the two sides could stage.

Paul was raised in a strict pharisaical setting, so it was naturally difficult for him to understand why the issue of idolatry would be bothering anyone. Before He came to salvation in Christ, he was "an Hebrew of the Hebrews" (Phil. 3:5), a Hebraism meaning the strictest Hebrew there was. No doubt he had never set foot in a pagan temple, never participated in a pagan worship service, and never owned an idol. He knew well the unrelenting mockery certain Old Testament passages level against idolatry. In Isaiah 44:9–20, for instance, the prophet asserts that idols are fashioned from one part of a tree while the remainder of the wood serves to fuel a fire for baking bread and roasting meat. The idolatrous worshiper is so foolish that he has forgotten that the idol he reverences is made of the same material that cooked his dinner! Undoubtedly Paul had nothing but scorn for worthless idols. That is why he could say in 1 Corinthians 8:4, "As concerning therefore the eating of those things that are offered in sacrifice unto idols, we know that an idol is nothing in the world, and that there is none other God but one." For Paul the answer to every question stemmed from having a correct view of theology. Central to his system of belief was the truth of Deuteronomy 6:4–5, a passage that commands man to love God with every aspect of his being because God is unique. There was no room for idols in Paul's heart.

Paul also realized, however, that many of the Christians at Corinth had grown up in an environment completely different from his. They had been steeped in idolatry,[22] and an idol was in their minds a physical representation of an actual deity with real personality and power. Salvation had brought deliverance from devotion to these false gods, but the Corinthian believers' background had a tendency to produce consciences so oversensitive that they thought eating food sacrificed to idols, no matter what the venue, was morally wrong: "For some with conscience of the idol unto this hour eat it as a thing offered unto an idol; and their conscience being weak is defiled" (1 Cor. 8:7).

Here is the crucial conclusion Paul reached when he considered the difference between his own conscience and the consciences of many in Corinth: under no circumstances would he do anything to encourage oversensitive believers to violate their consciences. Paul declares, "Wherefore, if meat make my brother to offend, I will eat no flesh while the world standeth, lest I make my brother to offend" (1 Cor. 8:13; see also Rom. 14:19–23). To violate the prohibitions of one's conscience is to sin, whether that conscience is oversensitive or not. Because Paul loved God, and his neighbor

---

[22]W. Harold Mare notes, "The importance of the question of 'foods offered in sacrifice to idols' (*eidolothuton*) becomes evident when one realizes how thoroughly idolatry and pagan sacrifices permeated all levels of Greek and Roman society. Indeed, people could hardly escape contact with the pagan practices and their influence." "1 Corinthians," in *The Expositor's Bible Commentary*, ed. Frank E. Gaebelein (Grand Rapids: Zondervan, 1976), 10:238. Samuel E. Horn agrees: "Daily, the Corinthian believers were forced to interact with paganism and idolaters. This pervasive interaction posed some serious problems for believers, especially in the area of idolatry. In short, how was a believer committed to the true God and commanded to eschew idolatry to interact in a society where every social or civic event, every religious holiday, and even meat sold in the marketplace was in some way associated with idolatry?" "A Biblical Theology of Christian Liberty: An Analysis of the Major Pauline Passages in Galatians, Colossians, I Corinthians, and Romans" (PhD diss., Bob Jones University, 1995), 103.

as himself (see Matt. 22:37–40), his conscience carefully regulated his liberty.

Apparently the situation in Corinth had degenerated to the point where some Christians, who shared Paul's view of idols, had actually gone so far as to dine at the venue of the idol's temple. Their consciences were not controlled by a heart of love for their fellow believers. "For if any man see thee which hast knowledge sit at meat in the idol's temple, shall not the conscience of him which is weak be emboldened to eat those things which are offered to idols; and through thy knowledge shall the weak brother perish, for whom Christ died?" (8:10–11). Paul then devoted all of 1 Corinthians 9 to the importance of denying one's own personal preferences in deference to others, lest there develop a hindrance to the proclamation of the gospel.[23]

Christians ought to be more concerned for the welfare of their brothers in Christ than for some freedom they think they have. They also ought to guard their testimony to the unsaved. I have noticed that unbelievers sometimes have a better idea about how Christians should act than Christians have! An unsaved person in Corinth no doubt would have been shocked to see someone claiming new life in Christ consuming food in an idol's temple, fresh from a pagan worship ritual.

Paul clearly denounced the practice of eating at the idol's temple (see 10:14–23). No person who enjoyed fellowship (*koinōnia*) with Christ should fellowship with demons (v. 20). But the question remained concerning a Christian's being invited to eat at the home of an unbeliever. Perhaps some believers in Corinth were refus-

---

[23]"Paul defends himself in a way that emphasizes his example of self-denial and foregoing of personal rights, the very virtues he has just called upon his readers to exercise." Randy Leedy, "To Eat or Not to Eat: The Issue Concluded," *Biblical Viewpoint* 32:1 (April 1998), 40.

ing the opportunity to dine with someone who needed to hear the gospel simply because the Christian was fearful of violating his oversensitive conscience. After all, perhaps the unbeliever would serve food that had been sacrificed to an idol. Paul insists that the believer should not refuse the opportunity to eat at an unbeliever's home. To avoid violating one's conscience, the believer should ask no questions concerning the origin of the food and just eat it (10:27)! If someone advises[24] that the food was offered to idols, however, the Christian should not eat it "for conscience sake" (v. 28). Then Paul adds, "Conscience, I say, not thine own, but the other" (v. 29).

Once again Paul returns to his emphasis from chapter 8 that a Christian should never lay a stumbling block in another person's path (8:9). Why should Paul give anyone an opportunity to denounce his freedom of conscience as injurious to others (vv. 29–30)? Paul has decided that the key issue is God's glory, not the insistence of doing something his conscience has deemed permissible (v. 31). Out of a heart of love for his fellow man, Paul shunned any action that would cause spiritual injury to anyone (vv. 32–33).

Paul's example of diligence in guarding his actions so that he does not violate anyone's conscience is rapidly being replaced in popular Christian literature these days by a decidedly different model—an independent, liberated lifestyle that is fixated on what the believer perceives as his rights. Notice what Charles Swindoll advises in determining how the Christian should live: "I like the way some saint of old put it: 'Love God with all your heart . . .

---

[24]Leedy maintains that the informant is another believer, not an unsaved person. "Paul nowhere else shows concern for the pagan conscience (though he does acknowledge that they have one, however much they abuse it); protecting the conscience is a strictly Christian concern" (p. 45). Mare concurs with this assessment: "If, however, at the dinner someone (probably a fellow Christian; cf. v. 29a) points out that the meat was offered to an idol, then the believer is to refrain from eating the meat" (p. 253).

then do as you please.' The healthy restraint is in the first phrase, the freedom is in the second. That's how to live a grace-oriented, liberated life."[25]

Such advice sounds quite liberating, but Swindoll never develops the concept of how love for God produces restraint. Any limits to one's liberty are left in a mystical realm of obscurity. Swindoll also seems to think that freedom from slavery to sin (Rom. 6) means freedom to live apart from conscience—especially from other people's consciences. After a largely profitable chapter describing the believer's freedom from slavery to sin,[26] Swindoll takes up the topic of guiding others to freedom. He asks if there is ever a time when a Christian should restrain his freedom, and Swindoll answers the question affirmatively. Then he declares, "But I must hasten to add that I believe such restraint is an individual matter. It is not to be legislated, not something to be forced on someone else. Limitations are appropriate and necessary, but I fail to find in Scripture any place where one is to require such restraint from another. To do so is legalism."[27]

By Swindoll's definition, Paul himself is a legalist. The whole idea of 1 Corinthians 8–10 is Paul's demand for Christians to act out of love in restraining the liberty their consciences grant them in certain actions that would harm the oversensitive brother or turn the unbeliever away from the gospel. Paul did not mince words in condemning the practice of eating meals at the temple of an idol: "The things which the Gentiles sacrifice, they sacrifice to devils, and not to God: and I would not that ye should have fellowship with devils. Ye cannot drink the cup of the Lord, and the cup of devils: ye cannot be partakers of the Lord's table, and of the table

---

[25]Swindoll, 20 (ellipsis original).

[26]Ibid., 103–122.

[27]Ibid., 127–28.

of devils" (10:20–21). Paul demanded abstinence from eating food that someone had specified as coming from a sacrifice to an idol. He insisted that believers restrain themselves from doing anything to wound the "weak" consciences of fellow believers.

The biblical model of conduct is balance between liberty to do something one's conscience allows and love for the brethren that willingly restricts personal freedom for the benefit of others. In order for the Christian's conscience to be neither weak nor libertine, the Holy Spirit must produce a wisdom in the believer's heart that stems from careful study, exegesis, and prayerful application of the Scripture. Obedience to the Word of God is ultimately the objective proof of whether or not one loves Christ (see John 14:15). Indeed, "knowledge puffeth up, but charity [love] edifieth" (1 Cor. 8:1).

Conscience ought to impel the Christian to imitate Paul's example. Since conscience is a function of the heart, that is where our focus must be. We cannot be content with simply adhering to outward standards of Christian conduct, as necessary as they may be. We must be training our children to internalize the Scripture, informing their hearts and consciences with correct theology.[28] We must encourage making decisions that are commensurate with the love for Christ we claim to have. Finally, we must avoid all idolatry and anything that brings us into contact with demonic influences. These forces of wickedness are as pervasive in our society as they were in Corinth in Paul's day. We may not have pagan temples, but we have conduits of demonic teaching and control. The print and television media daily spew ideas and images the demons have promoted. The Internet is a source not only of helpful information but also of material from the infernal regions. The believer

---

[28]For an excellent discussion of how 1 Cor. 8–10 applies to our day, see Leedy, 47–49.

must develop a spiritual discernment that stems from a biblically informed conscience.

CONSCIENCE PRODUCES GODLY LIVING

Internal, spiritual discernment must manifest itself in godly living. I was a Christian for a number of years before I realized this truth from my own study of Scripture. I have no pedigree as a fundamentalist, and the evangelical church in which I spent my early years as a believer did not emphasize the connection between the conscience and specific choices a Christian makes. During my undergraduate training at Syracuse University, I was a member of Campus Crusade for Christ. I still recall vividly the event that forced me to consider the necessity of allowing conscience to affect outward lifestyle decisions. As the weather at Syracuse changed from the arctic blasts of winter to the moderate temperatures of spring, the coeds at the university began to shed their heavy apparel for lighter, and significantly scantier, clothing. The resulting spectacle was not conducive to sanctification. One spring day my Campus Crusade group had a picnic, and some of the Christian girls arrived in attire that was just as revealing as what the majority of university coeds wore. When I suggested to the leader of our group that he or his wife talk to the young ladies who were dressed immodestly, he asked me when I had developed into a legalist! It was the first time I had ever heard the term, and it seemed to me that he had chosen an inappropriate way to sidestep the issue.

Paul never avoided discussing the relationship between his conscience and the godly living it produced. In Acts 24:1–27, Luke records the events of Paul's appearance before Felix. Although the historical record of Antonius Felix is incomplete, historians know enough about him to conclude that he had little regard for Roman justice and a high regard for greed.[29] The high priest, Ananias, together with a lawyer named Tertullus, brought charges against Paul before Felix. Tertullus asserted that Paul was "a pestilent fellow," stirring up strife among the Jews wherever he went (v. 5). He also accused Paul of desecrating the temple (v. 6).

One can hardly deny that Paul's preaching of the gospel routinely stirred up trouble, but the offense the message produced was the fault of those who heard it. Paul wished to see his countrymen come to faith in Christ, not riot. Concerning the charge that Paul had desecrated the temple, the truth was that he had brought four men under a vow of purification into the temple. But the Jews had mistakenly assumed that Paul had brought Trophimus the (Gentile) Ephesian in as well, simply because he had been seen earlier in Paul's company (see Acts 21:24–29).

Paul explained to Felix that his Jewish accusers could not prove any of the charges they were bringing against him (24:12–13). Then the apostle to the Gentiles declared, "And herein do I exercise myself, to have always a conscience void of offense toward God, and toward men" (v. 16). The phrase *void of offense* is the translation of the Greek adjective *aproskopos.* This adjective belongs to a family of Greek words that are all related to the concept of stumbling and the spiritual disaster that accompanies it. *Aproskopon suneidēsin* is "a conscience which has remained undefiled by sin."[30] Before the omniscient gaze of God and the evaluation of men, Paul's zealous aim was to live under the guidance of a conscience that motivated him to live undefiled by sin.

---

[29]See E. M. Blaiklock, "Felix, Antonius," in *The Zondervan Pictorial Encyclopedia of the Bible*, ed. Merrill C. Tenney (Grand Rapids: Zondervan, 1975–76), 2:526–28.

[30]J. Guhrt, "Offense, Scandal, Stumbling Block," in *The New International Dictionary of New Testament Theology*, ed. Colin Brown (Grand Rapids: Zondervan, 1976), 2:707.

Submission to a conscience that has been thoroughly informed by the Word of God is not merely an option for the believer to consider—it is absolutely mandatory. People who continually suppress the activity of conscience are walking a dangerous path. In one of the most sobering passages of warning in the New Testament, Paul told Timothy, "This charge I commit unto thee, son Timothy, according to the prophecies which went before on thee, that thou by them mightest war a good warfare; holding faith and a good conscience; which some having put away concerning faith have made shipwreck" (1 Tim. 1:18–19).[31]

Paul was personally familiar with shipwreck. In Acts 27:1–44 Luke devotes an entire chapter to a narrative about the shipwreck Paul experienced on his way to Rome. A fierce storm assailed the ship in which he was traveling, and the sailors found themselves completely unable to steer their own course. So they struck the sails, threw everything they could overboard, and resigned themselves to a watery grave. Only Paul's assurance that an angel had promised him no loss of life kept the men encouraged. Finally the ship ran aground on a sandbar, and the 276 passengers and crew made it to dry land. The ship and its cargo were a total loss.

With this image in mind, the interpreter can begin to formulate what a shipwreck of faith involves. When a person actively rejects faith and a good conscience as the compass of his life, the loss he sustains is devastating. In 1 Timothy 1:19 Paul says that faith, the doctrine a person holds regarding Christ and His atoning work (see 1 Tim. 1:15–17), is necessarily bound up with conscience—the internal judge of whether or not one's actions are commensurate with the doctrine he says he believes. When conscience smites one's inner being with guilt over sin, the person with saving faith

---

[31] Note the translation of v. 19 in the NASB: "Keeping faith and a good conscience, which some have rejected and suffered shipwreck in regard to their faith."

trusts the One Who is "faithful and just to forgive us our sins, and to cleanse us from all unrighteousness" (1 John 1:9). But to reject the operation of conscience is to hazard one's soul. It is possible for someone to have manifested an intellectual faith that is not the same as saving faith (see James 2:19) or an emotional faith that does not last through testing (see Matt. 13:20–21).[32] Rejecting the moral directives of Scripture and the condemnation that conscience brings to bear on such disobedience may demonstrate for all to see that a person never really had saving faith at all. Such was the case of Hymenaeus and Alexander (1 Tim. 1:20). Shipwreck is not a pretty sight.

CONSCIENCE IMPARTS CONFIDENCE

Of course Paul did not suspect that Timothy had less than saving faith.[33] Paul knew that the proper operation of conscience would impart a wonderful confidence in Timothy's heart that would sustain him through his Christian life and service. Paul had every expectation that Timothy would experience what he had found: "I thank God, whom I serve from my forefathers with pure conscience, that without ceasing I have remembrance of thee in my prayers night and day" (2 Tim. 1:3). The phrase *whom I serve from my forefathers* is a literal rendering, but the meaning is somewhat opaque. The Greek preposition *apo*, in addition to conveying the sense of separation from a place or point of origin, can also refer to the source of something.[34] The source of Paul's service is the knowledge of God he has received from his Jewish ancestors. Just as

---

[32] For a discussion of these aspects of belief that fall short of saving faith, see Augustus Hopkins Strong, *Systematic Theology* (Valley Forge, PA: The Judson Press, 1907), 837–38.

[33] See R. C. H. Lenski, *The Interpretation of St. Paul's Epistles to the Colossians, to the Thessalonians, to Timothy, to Titus and to Philemon* (Minneapolis: Augsburg, 1937), 533.

[34] See Bauer, 86–87.

faithful Israelites had worshiped God and passed His Word down to succeeding generations, so now Paul continues this service to God with a clean conscience. Just as the priest had to be ceremonially clean in his duties at the temple, so Paul's conscience was free from any impurity that would hinder his service for Christ.

Anyone who has ever preached or taught God's Word knows the experience of communicating a truth that has had a powerful, personal impact in his life. It is with tremendous confidence that a person can proclaim what has deeply touched his own heart. Paul had a great burden for his fellow Israelites, and in communicating that pressing weight he could assure the Roman believers, "I say the truth in Christ, I lie not, my conscience also bearing me witness in the Holy Ghost" (Rom. 9:1). Paul had saturated his heart with God's Word, and he knew the great promises the Lord had given His chosen people through the prophets. Most of Paul's Jewish brethren had hardened their hearts against the gospel and refused to see that Jesus was their Messiah. In God's providence, however, many Gentiles had gladly believed the good news of salvation by grace through faith. Did that mean God had rejected the Jew and chosen to fulfill His promises through the Gentile? Paul set about to communicate his antipathy to such an idea in Romans 9–11. With a conscience informed by the Scripture and illuminated by the Holy Spirit, Paul had great confidence in the irrevocable gifts and calling of God (11:29). Someday all Israel would be saved (v. 26). So great was the confidence Paul's conscience produced that he could truthfully say, "I could wish that myself were accursed from Christ for my brethren, my kinsmen according to the flesh" (9:3).

A good conscience produces the confidence necessary to stand for the Lord against all opposition. In 1 Peter 3:16, Peter admonishes believers who are suffering righteously for their faith to have a good conscience, so that "whereas they speak evil of you, as of evildoers, they may be ashamed that falsely accuse your good conversation in Christ." Peter knew the grief of heart that resulted from being a hypocritical disciple of Christ. After Judas had betrayed Christ and the Roman soldiers had arrested Him, Peter had followed Him to the courtyard of the high priest. Three times he had denied having any acquaintance with Jesus, and the rooster had crowed in fulfillment of the prophecy Christ had spoken. Peter had wept bitterly as his conscience condemned him for his act of disloyalty (Matt. 26:69–75).

Peter learned the hard way that confidence in service for the Master comes only from a conscience that is fully assured of Who Christ is and what He has promised. Of course Peter found forgiveness and restoration from His gracious Savior. He learned the importance of making sure there is no validity to the slanderous charges of unsaved people against a believer's lifestyle. We must guard our testimonies at work, in the home, and wherever we encounter people who need to see a genuine devotion to Christ. Only a clear conscience produces an unflinching testimony for Christ that no one can silence.

CONSCIENCE FURTHERS THE DEVELOPMENT OF LOVE

The most important role of conscience, however, is found in a crucial verse related to Paul's philosophy of ministry: "Now the end of the commandment is charity out of a pure heart, and of a good conscience, and of faith unfeigned" (1 Tim. 1:5). Whenever Paul writes about the *telos* ("end") of something, it is time for the reader to sit up and pay close attention. This Greek word conveys the idea of a goal, purpose, or outcome.[35] It describes the outcome Paul wished to see his preaching produce. He specifies this goal as love (*agapē*).

Agapē is not emotional sentimentality. It is a sacrificial attitude and volitional action that works for the best for another person,

---

[35] Ibid., 819.

regardless of any personal cost. It is altruistic and generous. Love is best understood at the foot of the Cross: "But God commendeth his love toward us, in that, while we were yet sinners, Christ died for us" (Rom. 5:8). The fact that we can even comprehend this sort of love is due to Christ's demonstrating it to us by becoming the propitiation for our sins (1 John 4:9–10). Paul devoted the entirety of 1 Corinthians 13 to describe this most important of Christian virtues. Love is more important than any spiritual gift God has graciously given us. Without it we are nothing. Love is patient, kind, and humble. It is even greater than faith and hope. It is the essence of the entire teaching of the Old Testament (Matt. 22:40). The highest motivation for everything we do in the Christian life is love. Paul declared in 2 Corinthians 5:14–15, "For the love of Christ constraineth us; because we thus judge, that if one died for all, then were all dead: and that he died for all, that they which live should not henceforth live unto themselves, but unto him which died for them, and rose again."

In 1 Timothy 1:5 Paul informs us not only about the primary importance of love in his ministry but also about how God develops love in the believer's life. Love issues from a pure heart, a good conscience, and genuine faith. The mark of spiritual growth is an internal cleansing of the heart by the pure water of God's Word. We all enter the Christian life with the same selfish motivations and thoughts that drive human existence. Then Scripture declares to us the sacrificial love of Christ that resulted in His death on the cross in our behalf. Through the Bible we learn that we are no longer our own because we have been purchased at the cost of the blood of Christ (1 Cor. 6:19–20). Now we must have a radically different view of life. Our lives are not our own to direct. Life no longer consists of an insane quest to accumulate all the wealth we can before death parts us from our treasures. No longer do we view sensuality and extremely stimulating experiences as the highest good of existence. Now we desire to live for the glory of Christ and the edification of fellow believers. Love begins to transform our lives from the inside out.

The judge of whether we are growing in love is the conscience. Conscience is not something to fear. Yes, it produces guilt when we transgress God's Word, but that guilt should cause repentance and restoration to fellowship with our loving Savior. Conscience is like a cattle prod impelling us ever forward toward growth in the image of Christ. Conscience shows us the need to love the Bible and treasure its words in our hearts. This guardian of the heart evaluates the quality of our faith and shows us whether there is any hypocrisy in our lives. Every one of us is prone to believe and say one thing but live in a different manner. The prophet Jeremiah lamented the deplorable condition of the human heart when he wrote, "The heart is deceitful above all things, and desperately wicked: who can know it?" (Jer. 17:9). A scripturally informed conscience shows us where we have deceived ourselves. It is easy for us to think we love the Lord, when our hearts are actually far from Him. We are prone to take the liberty that God has given us and turn it into license for selfish, worldly living.

4

THE NATURE OF TRUE LIBERTY

Genuine liberty is the ability to live the way God has planned, not the way Satan's world system has programmed people. It seems that many Christians these days are quite concerned to fit in with the spirit of the age. A good illustration of this accommodation is found in a small section of *A Survey of Old Testament Introduction* by Gleason L. Archer Jr. Archer takes a good, conservative position on almost every issue he covers in the book. When he discusses creation, however, Archer adopts the view that each day of creation in Genesis 1 is actually a geologic age. He is forthright about his motivation in seeing each "day" as millions of years:

> From a superficial reading of Genesis 1, the impression would seem to be that the entire creative process took place in six twenty-four-hour days. If this was the true intent of the Hebrew author (a questionable deduction, as will be presently shown), this seems to run counter to modern scientific research, which indicates that the planet Earth was created several billion years ago.[1]

In other words, Archer is more concerned with what modern science has concluded than he is about the plain words of Genesis 1. This method of imposing a cultural grid that determines what Scripture must mean is also apparent in the area of Christian liberty. Americans these days manifest an increasing dislike for being

[1]Gleason L. Archer, *A Survey of Old Testament Introduction*, revised and expanded ed. (Chicago: Moody, 1994), 196.

told what to do. To drive at the speed limit on an interstate highway, for example, is to make oneself a hazard to most of the other cars traveling at almost unbelievably fast speeds. The speed-limit sign becomes an unwelcome intrusion into a driver's plans to arrive at his destination in as short a time period as possible. Americans have seemingly lost the important concept of liberty in law. I am free to drive anywhere in the United States I desire, but I must obey traffic laws while I am driving. Laws regulate liberty so that my freedom does not impinge on another person's rights. When a traffic light turns red, my freedom to make progress toward my destination temporarily ceases. To ignore the red light invites loss of property or life as I crash into a vehicle that has the right of way. Some Christians have adopted the antipathy our culture has toward rules and have applied this skewed idea to the realm of Christian liberty. Charles Swindoll, for example, asserts,

> More and more Christians are realizing that the man-made restrictions and legalistic regulations under which they have been living have not come from the God of grace, but have been enforced by people who do not want others to be free. It is not an overstatement to describe this movement as an awakening that is beginning to sweep across the country. Nothing could please me more. This awakening to freedom is long overdue. It fits the times in which we are living.[2]

It would seem that much of evangelicalism has become so culturally relevant that it has ceased to have a distinctive identity. Swindoll seems more concerned with making the Bible fit "the times in which we are living" than he is with letting the Bible speak its

---

[2]Swindoll, xiii.

inspired message—no matter how it cuts across the grain of cultural expectation.

TRUE LIBERTY INCLUDES RESTRAINT

The biblical concept of liberty does not fit our hedonistic culture well at all. Just as true liberty in the political realm is based on the restraint of law, so spiritually the believer is subject to the law of Christ: "But whoso looketh into the *perfect law of liberty*, and continueth therein, he being not a forgetful hearer, but a doer of the work, this man shall be blessed in his deed" (James 1:25, emphasis added). The word translated "liberty" in this verse is the Greek word *eleutheria*. In secular Greek culture *eleutheria* was freedom from slavery to enjoy the full rights of citizenship. "But in order to preserve this freedom, the law is required as the principle of order. Freedom and law are thus not contradictory opposites. They belong together and qualify each other."[3]

The New Testament never uses the term *eleutheria* to describe political freedom, but quite clearly James 1:25 declares that the Christian enjoys a spiritual freedom that includes restraint. "The perfect law of liberty" for the Christian is vastly different from bondage to the performance-based religion the Pharisees promoted. Christ has redeemed us from the death that the Mosaic law demanded for transgressors, and now we have a new Master. Sin was our previous, cruel owner, but Christ has borne our sin in His body on the tree. Through faith in His vicarious atonement, we are free from the curse of having to meet the standard of God's righteousness by our own works. Paul commands us to "stand fast therefore in the liberty wherewith Christ hath made us free, and be not entangled again with the yoke of bondage" (Gal. 5:1). Christ's truth has set us free (see John 8:32) to live in obedience to God's will by

---

[3]J. Blunck, "Freedom," in *The New International Dictionary of New Testament Theology*, ed. Colin Brown (Grand Rapids: Zondervan, 1975), 1:715.

a power the Mosaic law could never impart. "When Jas. 1:25 and 2:12 speak of the 'law of freedom,' *eleutheria* means the new way of life in which a man lives in accordance with the will of God."[4]

Out of a heart of love for what the Savior has done for us, we now are careful not to use "liberty for an occasion to the flesh, but by love [to] serve one another" (Gal. 5:13). This new life of liberty is possible only as we "walk in the Spirit," and then we will "not fulfil the lust of the flesh" (v. 16). J. Blunck states this truth well: "Man's true freedom does not consist of the unfettered power to direct his life, either in a political or in a Stoic sense. It lies in life with God, lived as it was originally intended by God for man."[5] Empowered by the Holy Spirit of God, the believer now has the ability to accomplish the will of God: "For so is the will of God, that with well doing ye may put to silence the ignorance of foolish men: as free, and not using your liberty as a cloke of maliciousness, but as the servants of God" (1 Pet. 2:15–16). Once we were the servants of sin, but now we are the slaves (*douloi*) of God. Freedom for the Christian is found in loving submission to the Savior's will and in thankful empowerment for living as we ought, not license to live as we please.

TRUE LIBERTY PRODUCES INCREASING KNOWLEDGE OF CHRIST

Back in the days when I was in Campus Crusade for Christ, I sometimes heard students who professed faith in Christ attempt to justify their worldly behavior with the motto "Where the Spirit of the Lord is, there is liberty" (2 Cor. 3:17). These students thought liberty was freedom to have the best of both worlds—enjoyment of salvation and essentially the same lifestyle as their unsaved counterparts. Of course such an idea can be derived only if the

---

[4]Ibid., 717.

[5]Ibid., 718.

reader takes 2 Corinthians 3:17 completely out of its context. One of the most important rules of hermeneutics is to interpret a verse within its context. By ignoring this cardinal rule, the interpreter may make the Bible mean virtually anything he wants it to say. An examination of context shows that 2 Corinthians 3:17 is a wonderful promise of the believer's liberty to grow in the knowledge of Christ through the agency of the Holy Spirit.

Paul's meaning in 2 Corinthians 3 can be understood correctly only as the interpreter takes into account the antecedent theology of Exodus 33 and 34. In Exodus 33:12–17, Moses pleaded with the Lord not to take His presence away from the nation of Israel— even though the people had just displayed horrendous rebellion in the golden-calf incident. God promised Moses that His presence would go up with Israel to Canaan. Moses was not content, however, with simply a general knowledge of God displayed in the pillar of cloud by day and fire by night. He wanted the Lord to display His glory to him (v. 18). When someone today thinks of God's glory, he thinks of an ethereal brightness. Although this is certainly one aspect of God's glory, Exodus 34 shows us that the foundational meaning of the term involves the entirety of God's revealed attributes.

Exodus 34:5–7 recounts the Lord's answer to Moses' prayer for an understanding of the divine glory. "And the Lord descended in the cloud, and stood with him there, and proclaimed the name of the Lord" (v. 5). In order to understand this statement, one has to realize that the "name" in Hebrew usage is a description of a person's character.[6] So when the Lord proclaimed His name, He

---

[6]Walter C. Kaiser notes, "The concept of personal names in the OT often included existence, character, and reputation (I Sam. 25:25). . . . The name of God also signifies the whole self-disclosure of God in his holiness and truth." *"shem,"* in *Theological Wordbook of the Old Testament*, ed. R. Laird Harris (Chicago: Moody, 1980), 2:934.

was describing His character to Moses. He is "the Lord, the Lord God" (v. 6). The name *LORD* is not simply a moniker He wants man to call Him. As His appearance to Moses at the burning bush had shown (Exod. 3:13–15), this divine name is a statement of His ability to meet His people's needs. It communicates His closeness to His people and His desire for a covenantal relationship with them.[7] The name *Lord God* conveys both God's immanence and His transcendence. Next the Lord revealed to Moses that He is "merciful and gracious, longsuffering, and abundant in goodness and truth" (v. 6). Even without a detailed discussion of the meaning of all these terms that tell us what God is like, the reader can understand clearly that God's glory is the honor of His revealed attributes. Moses' request to see God's glory was a plea to know Him better.

When Moses came down from the mountain after forty days in God's presence, he did not realize that his face radiated the glory of God (Exod. 34:29). This sight frightened his fellow Israelites, but Moses let the glory of God shine from his countenance as he recounted the words God had communicated in the law. Then Moses placed a veil over his face until the next time he went into the tent of meeting to speak with the Lord (vv. 30–35). The reader of the narrative in Exodus 34 is left to draw his own conclusions about why Moses would put the veil over his face *after* he was done speaking to his people (Exod. 34:33, NASB). It must be that his action was not designed to prevent fear in people's hearts, but Moses' real motivation remains a mystery.

With this background in mind, Paul informs his readers why it was that Moses veiled his face: he did not want the Israelites to see the glory fade (2 Cor. 3:13). Then Paul makes an interesting

---

[7]See J. Barton Payne, *The Theology of the Older Testament* (Grand Rapids: Zondervan, 1962), 147–49.

application of this Old Testament passage for his day. He asserts that a veil still prevents his countrymen from understanding the person of Christ. Only when someone turns to Christ for salvation does God remove the veil from his heart (vv. 14–16). The removal of the veil takes place by the agency of the Holy Spirit, for "where the Spirit of the Lord is, there is liberty" (v. 17). In context, 2 Corinthians 3:17 refers to the liberty the New Testament believer enjoys in understanding the revelation of Christ's glory as He has revealed Himself in the Scripture. As a Christian beholds the glory of the Lord with unveiled face, he is transformed step by step by the Spirit into the glorious image he sees. This is spiritual metamorphosis (v. 18). True liberty allows the believer to see Christ as He is and to grow in the ability to reflect Christ's image to a world that is perishing in sin.

5

CONCLUSION

We have seen that some evangelical leaders today are confusing God's people with a redefinition of *legalism*. Historically the term has referred to adding works of the law to God's grace in an attempt to earn salvation. The redefined *legalism* is an undue emphasis on external guidelines for Christian living resulting in preoccupation with outward performance instead of inward reality. This redefinition certainly describes an aberrant view of sanctification, but the way some proponents are using the new definition tends to give Christians the idea that only internal heart matters are of real consequence. The result is a devaluation of the correspondence between what the Christian believes and how he actually lives. A transformed heart must result in a transformed lifestyle.

Biblical standards are of utmost importance in the process of sanctification, as long as one views these standards as a necessary function of the Christian's scripturally informed conscience. The conscience can, indeed, be oversensitive ("weak," as Paul describes the condition). But as we allow the Word of God to transform our minds, we find that conscience is the true guardian of our hearts. To act in violation of conscience is to invite horrific spiritual loss. We have been set at liberty not to act as we please but to live under the perfect law of liberty.

Unsaved people must see a correct reflection of Christ's character in our lives. The problem in our day is not that Christians need liberation from supposed "legalistic" standards of conduct so that they may live like chameleons, blending seamlessly into a worldly culture. We must not think that we have to live like the world in order to win the world to Christ. Instead, we need to interpret the Bible well and internalize its truth so that the gospel transforms our lives. Those who are in Christ must enjoy the liberty to love and obey God out of a heart that is governed by a scripturally informed conscience.

Just as God justified the believer by grace through faith, so He is currently sanctifying him. There is no room for boasting in human merit or attainment. I can do nothing to make myself more accepted in the Beloved than I was at the moment God saved my eternal soul. But I must not think that on account of my positional righteousness in Christ my lifestyle does not matter to the Lord. He has graciously given me the Scripture to educate my conscience. Every day I make countless decisions about what to think, say, and act that must issue from a properly informed conscience. I must allow conscience to guard my heart, judge my actions, produce godly living, and develop my love for God and my fellow man. I find true, biblical liberty only as I submit myself to the standards of God's Word.